Unless the Lord Builds the Church

Unless the Lord Builds the Church

by
John MacArthur, Jr.

"GRACE TO YOU"
P.O. Box 4000
Panorama City, CA   91412

©1991 by
JOHN F. MACARTHUR, JR.

All Scripture quotations, unless noted otherwise, are from the *New Scofield Reference Bible*, King James Version. Copyright © 1967 by Oxford University Press, Inc. Reprinted by permission.

Moody Press, a ministry of the Moody Bible Institute, is designed for education, evangelization, and edification. If we may assist you in knowing more about Christ and the Christian life, please write us without obligation: Moody Press, c/o MLM, Chicago, Illinois, 60610.

ISBN: 0-8024-5332-5

1 2 3 4 5 Printing/LC/Year 95 94 93 92 91

Printed in the United States of America

Contents

These Bible studies are taken from messages delivered by Pastor-Teacher John MacArthur, Jr., at Grace Community Church in Sun Valley, California. These messages have been combined into a four-tape album titled *Unless the Lord Builds the Church*. You may purchase this series either in an attractive vinyl cassette album or as individual cassettes. To purchase these tapes, request the album *Unless the Lord Builds the Church*, or ask for the tapes by their individual GC numbers. Please consult the current price list; then send your order, making your check payable to:

"GRACE TO YOU"
P.O. Box 4000
Panorama City, CA 91412

Or call the following toll-free number:
1-800-55-GRACE

1

The Supreme Confession

Outline

Introduction

Lesson
I.   The Setting (v. 13*a*)
II. The Examination (vv. 13*b*-15)
     A. The Wrong Answers
        1. John the Baptist
        2. Elijah
        3. Jeremiah
        4. One of the prophets
     B. The Right Answer
III. The Confession (v. 16)
     A. Initially
        1. The disciples' affirmation of Christ
        2. The disciples' doubts about Christ
     B. Later on
        1. Christ is the Messiah
        2. Christ is the Son of the Living God
IV. The Source (v. 17)
V.   The Evidence (v. 17)
     A. The Words of Christ
     B. The Works of Christ
     C. The Lordship of Christ
        1. Stated
        2. Illustrated
VI. The Result (v. 17)

Introduction

Jesus asked His disciples, "Who say ye that I am?" (Matt. 16:15). That question is the apex of Matthew's gospel and the thesis of both the Old and New Testaments. For more than two years Christ had been establishing, affirming, and building His disciples' confidence and commitment until Peter, on behalf of all the disciples, could give this supreme confession: "Thou art the Christ, the Son of the living God" (v. 16). That confession embodies the essence of true Christianity. Let's examine it more closely.

Lesson

I. THE SETTING (v. 13*a*)

"Jesus came into the borders of Caesarea Philippi."

For some months Christ had secluded Himself from misguided multitudes who wanted to make Him a political ruler, from King Herod, who wanted to kill Him out of jealous ambition, and from the Jewish leaders, who viewed Him as a threat to their religious system. He used that time to personally instruct His twelve disciples about the cross and other important spiritual matters.

During that time of seclusion Christ and His disciples had gone north of Galilee to Caesarea Philippi. After praying, Christ walked with His disciples along a road between some of the suburban villages of Caesarea Philippi (Mark 8:27; Luke 9:18). As they walked along, Christ asked His disciples two questions.

II. THE EXAMINATION (vv. 13*b*-15)

"He asked His disciples, saying, Who do men say that I, the Son of man, am? And they said, Some say that thou art John the Baptist; some, Elijah; and others, Jeremiah or one of the prophets. He saith unto them, But who say ye that I am?"

"Son of man" was the Lord's most common designation of Himself. Although it's a prophetic title referring to the Messiah (Dan. 7:13), Christ used it here as a sign of His identification with humanity. Christ had been preaching, teaching, and doing miracles for more than two years in revealing Himself to the world. In light of that self-revelation, it seems Christ's questions weren't for the purpose of finding out information, because He already knew what everyone believed. Rather, Christ wanted to contrast the wrong opinions of the populace against what would be the true confession of His disciples.

A. The Wrong Answers

1. John the Baptist

In response to Christ's first question the disciples noted that many people mistook Christ for John the Baptist. Matthew 14 says, "Herod, the tetrarch, heard of the fame of Jesus, and said unto his servants, This is John the Baptist; he is risen from the dead, and therefore mighty works do show forth themselves in him" (vv. 1-2). Those words represented popular opinion, not just Herod's. Herod had beheaded John the Baptist, who served as the forerunner of Christ, and now was afraid John had come back to spite him.

2. Elijah

Others thought Christ was the prophet Elijah. Many Jewish people expected Elijah to return to them prior to the Messiah's coming. That expectation was based on Malachi 4:5: "Behold, I will send you Elijah, the prophet, before the coming of the great and terrible day of the Lord."

3. Jeremiah

Still others thought Christ was the prophet Jeremiah. That popular opinion was based on a story about him in the Apocrypha (nonbiblical writings). According to the legend, Jeremiah took the Ark of the Covenant and altar of incense out of the Temple to prevent their desecration during the Babylonian Captivity (2 Maccabees 2:1-7). The legend also says that Jeremiah would return to restore the Temple items prior to the establishment of the messianic kingdom.

Second Maccabees goes on to say that Jeremiah gave a golden sword to Judas Maccabeus, who used it in leading the Maccabean revolution against the Greeks (15:15-16). Because of those legends, the Jews in the days of Christ looked upon Jeremiah as a hero.

4. One of the prophets

The general opinion that Christ was one of the prophets was also a popular view. Maybe people thought Christ was the prophet Zephaniah because of His warm spirit of love, but we really have no way of knowing which prophets they were thinking of. A parallel account in Luke 9:19 says that some thought he was one of the old prophets risen again. That provided people with an erroneous explanation for the supernatural abilities of Christ.

All those wrong answers have this in common: the people thought Jesus was the forerunner of the Messiah, not the Messiah Himself. They attempted to explain His supernatural powers by concluding He was a prophet. Likewise, many today say Jesus was a great man, but they won't personally embrace Him as Savior and Lord.

B. The Right Answer

Having heard the wrong opinions of the general populace, Christ now wanted to hear what the disciples had to say. So He asked, "But who say ye that I am?" (v. 15). Peter's response (v. 16) was an official and formal confession for all the disciples. Peter often served as the spokesman for the Twelve (Matt. 15:15; 19:27; 26:35, 40-41; John 6:68). It seems he had the ability to articulate what the disciples were thinking as a group.

III. THE CONFESSION (v. 16)

"Simon Peter answered and said, Thou art the Christ, the Son of the living God."

The Greek term translated "Christ" means "Messiah," or "Anointed One." The confession of the disciples was decisive, emphatic, and brief: Christ is the Messiah. But what did the disciples believe about Christ during the early part of His ministry?

A. Initially

1. The disciples' affirmation of Christ

Initially the disciples acknowledged that Christ was the Messiah (cf. John 1:41). They believed the testimony of John the Baptist, who said, "Behold the Lamb of God, who taketh away the sin of the world. . . . I saw, and bore witness that [Christ] is the Son of God" (John 1:29, 34). The disciples' initial belief was strengthened by their firsthand observations of Christ's supernatural abilities (vv. 47-48). And if Christ had planned to destroy the Roman Empire and set up His own earthly kingdom, it is likely the disciples would have given Him their full allegiance.

2. The disciples' doubts about Christ

However, when Christ became the object of hatred, rejection, and humiliation, the disciples began to wonder if their initial affirmation about Christ was correct. Even John the Baptist, the forerunner of Christ, had some doubts about His identity (Matt. 11:1-4).

During Christ's early ministry, the disciples had moments not only of great faith (cf. John 6:68) but also of little faith (cf. Matt. 8:26). Christ realized the need for personally instructing them to keep their faith from wavering. So He did just that.

B. Later on

1. Christ is the Messiah

By the time of the account in Matthew 16 our Lord had been teaching His disciples for more than two years. They had seen His miracles and heard His profound teaching. By this point they had a genuine belief that Christ was the Messiah. Although their understanding about His atoning work on the cross was incomplete, they recognized Christ to be the fulfillment of their hopes and the source of their salvation.

2. Christ is the Son of the living God

The Greek term translated "Son" speaks of essence, not servitude. By saying Christ is "the Son of the living God," the disciples were confessing that Christ is of the same essence as God. Christ Himself said He was equal with God (John 5:17-18). He is the "living God" as opposed to the dead idols that men vainly worship.

IV. THE SOURCE (v. 17)

"Jesus answered and said unto him, Blessed art thou, Simon Bar-jona; for flesh and blood hath not revealed it unto thee, but my Father, who is in heaven."

"Flesh and blood" is symbolic for humanness. "Simon" was Peter's name before his conversion, and Christ used it to point out the inadequacy and blindness of human reason in and of itself. It wasn't through human intellect or merit that Peter confessed Christ to be the Messiah. After all, "no man can say that Jesus is Lord, but by the Holy Spirit" (1 Cor. 12:3). Only God can reveal His Son to the human mind. Jesus said, "No man knoweth the Son, but the Father; neither knoweth any man the Father, except the Son, and he to whomsoever the Son will reveal him" (Matt. 11:27). Only by divine revelation can we know Christ.

As Christ personally instructed the disciples over a period of years, the Holy Spirit revealed to them that Jesus was the Messiah. Today the Holy Spirit continues to reveal the Son to those who hear Christ's teaching in Scripture, for "faith cometh by hearing, and hearing by the word of God" (Rom. 10:17). As you behold the glory of the Christ in Scripture, you'll be "changed into the same image from glory to glory, even as by the Spirit of the Lord" (2 Cor. 3:18).

V. THE EVIDENCE (v. 17)

Christ's words and works clearly reveal Him to be God.

A. The Words of Christ

   1. Matthew 7:22—"Many will say to me in that day, Lord, Lord." Christ is the Lord of judgment.

   2. Matthew 5:17—"Think not that I am come to destroy the law, or the prophets; I am not come to destroy, but to fulfill." Christ's authority and teaching are divine.

B. The Works of Christ

   1. Matthew 8:3—"Jesus put forth his hand, and touched him, saying, I will; be thou clean. And immediately his leprosy was cleansed." Here we see Christ's power over disease.

   2. Matthew 8:26—Christ "rebuked the winds and the sea; and there was a great calm." Here we see Christ's power over nature.

   3. Matthew 8:32—Christ commanded demons to come out of two people. When the demons came out, they went into a herd of swine, which then plunged into the sea and drowned. Here we see Christ's power over demons.

   4. Matthew 9:6—"That ye may know that the Son of man hath power on earth to forgive sins (then saith he to the sick of the palsy), Arise, take up thy bed,

and go unto thine house." This reveals Christ's power over sin.

5. Matthew 9:25—The daughter of a certain ruler lay dead. Christ went to her and "took her by the hand, and the maid arose." This reveals Christ's power over death.

C. The Lordship of Christ

Recognizing Jesus as Lord gave the disciples a fuller understanding about His being the Messiah.

1. Stated

Christ said He was "Lord even of the sabbath day" (Matt. 12:8). That statement places Christ beyond the realm of John the Baptist, Elijah, Jeremiah, or any other prophet. But to understand why, you need to know some things about the Sabbath.

Understanding the Sabbaths

The Sabbath, the seventh day of the week, was the center of life in Israel. In fact the Jewish religious calendar was set up in cycles of sevens. The Greek term translated "sabbath" means "rest" or "cessation." Primarily the Sabbath was a time to rest from physical labor and worship God. There were many Sabbaths for the Jewish people to observe.

1. The weekly Sabbath (Lev. 23:1-3)

The Jewish people regarded Saturday as the seventh day of the week. Every Saturday the people rested from their work and gathered for worship. That day was patterned after God's rest from His work of creation (Ex. 20:8-11) and served as a reminder of God's deliverance of Israel from Egypt (Deut. 5:12-15).

14

2. The Passover (vv. 4-8)

On the fourteenth day of Nisan (the first month of the year in the Jewish religious calendar) a prescribed meal was eaten in commemoration of the first Passover in Egypt. A central feature of this holy observance was the slaying of an unblemished lamb. Immediately following the Passover, the Jewish nation observed the Feast of Unleavened Bread, in part by offering numerous sacrifices each day and also by setting aside the first and seventh days for rest and worship.

3. The Feast of Firstfruits (vv. 9-14)

This observance took place seven weeks following the Feast of Unleavened Bread, on the fiftieth day. Because it was closely associated with the agricultural harvest, it is also called the Feast of Harvest. This was a one-day observance. No work was allowed, and numerous offerings were made.

4. The Feast of Trumpets (vv. 23-25)

This feast took place in the seventh month of the Jewish religious calendar. There were many animal sacrifices and much trumpet blowing.

5. The Day of Atonement (vv. 26-32)

This was observed on the tenth day of the seventh month. Only on this day did the high priest enter the Holy of Holies, symbolizing the necessity of atonement for sin. No person was to work, and all were to fast.

6. The Feast of Tabernacles (vv. 33-43)

During this feast the Jewish people lived in tents or booths (made of tree branches) in commemoration of Israel's manner of life during the wilderness journey from Egypt. The feast began in the seventh month of the religious calendar.

7. The Sabbath year (25:1-7)

Every seven years the people were to refrain from working their land or pruning their vines. The yield from the land was to be shared with the poor, servants, and visitors.

8. The Year of Jubilee (vv. 8-55)

After seven consecutive sabbatical years (forty-nine years), a special yearlong Jubilee was observed. The land was to lie fallow once again. During the year, lost inheritances were restored, slaves who so wished were set free, and former property could either be repurchased or automatically returned.

The Sabbaths were symbolic of the rest and holiness salvation brings through Christ. Just as the Old Testament sacrifices pointed to the Lamb of God, so also the whole Sabbath system pointed to Christ, who gives ultimate rest and holiness.

2. Illustrated

Christ "came to Nazareth, where he had been brought up; and, as his custom was, he went into the synagogue on the sabbath day, and stood up to read. And there was delivered unto him the book of the prophet Isaiah. And when he had opened the book, he found the place where it was written, The Spirit of the Lord is upon me, because he hath anointed me to preach the gospel to the poor; he hath sent me to heal the brokenhearted, to preach deliverance to the captives, and recovering of sight to the blind, to set at liberty them that are bruised, to preach the acceptable year of the Lord. . . . And [Christ] began to say unto them, This day is this Scripture fulfilled in your ears" (Luke 4:16-19, 21; cf. Isa. 61:1-2).

In reading Isaiah's prophecy Christ was saying, "I am the true Sabbath rest, the One who proclaims a spiritual Jubilee by freeing sinners from bondage to sin." That's why Christ said, "Come unto me, all ye that labor and are heavy laden, and I will give you rest" (Matt. 11:28). Through His atoning work on the cross, Christ inaugurated a new covenant, which did away with the sabbatical system (Col. 2:16-17). The righteous have entered Christ's salvation rest and look forward to ultimate rest in His presence (Heb. 4:9-11).

VI.   THE RESULT (v. 17)

"Blessed art thou, Simon Bar-jona."

The Lord's blessing is the bestowal of all His divine resources on the righteous. The righteous are blessed "with all spiritual blessings in heavenly places in Christ" (Eph. 1:3). If you truly confess Christ as the Messiah, the Son of the living God, and embrace Him as your own, you will enjoy His eternal and holy rest.

Focusing on the Facts

1.   Why did Christ occasionally seek seclusion from the crowds (see p. 8)?
2.   What does "Son of Man" in Matthew 16:13 mean (see p. 8)?
3.   Why does Christ question His disciples (see p. 9)?
4.   What was the opinion of King Herod and many others about Christ (see p. 9)?
5.   Why did many think Christ was the prophet Jeremiah (see p. 9)?
6.   What did all the wrong opinions have in common? How do those opinions compare with people's thinking today (see p. 10)?
7.   What did the twelve think about Christ during the early part of His ministry (see pp. 10-11)?
8.   How did Christ help keep the disciples' faith from wavering (see p. 11)?
9.   What does "the Son of the living God" mean (Matt. 16:16; see p. 11)?
10.   Why does Christ address Peter as "Simon" in verse 17 (see p. 12)?
11.   How did God reveal Christ to the twelve? How does He reveal His Son today (see pp. 12-13)?

12. What do the words and works of Christ reveal (see pp. 13-14)?
13. Why did the Jewish people rest from their work (Lev. 23:1-3; see p. 14)?
14. What did the Sabbaths symbolize (see p. 15)?
15. What was the significance of Christ's reading from Isaiah 61 (see p. 15)?
16. What specific blessing does the Lord bestow on the righteous (Eph. 1:3; see p. 16)?

Pondering the Principles

1. Christ is the true Sabbath rest. The salvation rest believers experience in Christ has been captured in Fanny Crosby's hymn "Safe in the Arms of Jesus":

    Safe in the arms of Jesus, safe on His gentle breast,
    There by His love o'ershaded, sweetly my soul shall rest.
    Hark! 'tis the voice of angels, borne in a song to me,
    Over the field of glory, over the jasper sea.

    Safe in the arms of Jesus, safe from corroding care,
    Safe from the world's temptations, sin cannot harm me
        there.
    Free from the blight of sorrow, free from my doubts
    and fears;
    Only a few more trials, only a few more tears!

    Jesus, my heart's dear refuge, Jesus has died for me;
    Firm on the Rock of Ages, ever my trust shall be.
    Here let me wait with patience, wait till the night is o'er;
    Wait till I see the morning break on the golden shore.

    Christ said, "Come unto me, all ye that labor and are heavy laden, and I will give you rest" (Matt. 11:28). Have you accepted the salvation rest Christ offers? If Christ is your Savior, thank and praise Him for the salvation rest He has given you.

2. On the Day of Pentecost Peter preached that God made Jesus "both Lord and Christ" (Acts 2:36). Peter willingly confessed Christ before others. Christ said, "Whosoever,

18

therefore, shall confess me before men, him will I confess also before my Father who is in heaven" (Matt. 10:32). Telling the lost about Christ is a mark of the true believer. Are you a witness for Christ? Be involved in the lives of your family, neighbors, and co-workers so that they can hear and see Christ.

2
The Church That Christ Builds—Part 1

Outline

Introduction
A. The Discouragement of the Disciples
B. The Persecution of the Disciples

Lesson
I. The Certainty of the Church's Existence
   A. Because of the Divine Method
   B. Because of the Divine Builder
   C. Because of the Divine Goal
II. The Intimacy Between Christ and His People
   A. In the New Testament
   B. In the Old Testament
III. The Identity of Those in the Church

Conclusion

Introduction

The heart of Matthew 16:13-20 is Christ's statement "I will build my church" (v. 18). Everything else in the passage amplifies that great statement.

Identifying the Church's Builder

Years ago someone was trying to find out why particular churches experienced great growth. That person visited my office and said, "All across the country I have found that large churches have leaders who desire to build the church. I want to ask you the same question I have asked them: Do you have a great desire to build the church?" I answered—much to his surprise—that I had no desire to build the church because Christ said He would do that. It's comforting to know that the building of the church doesn't depend on people, gimmicks, or programs. The Lord is the only Builder, and it's our joy as Christians to be a part of what He's building.

A. The Discouragement of the Disciples

Christ's promise to build His church came as the disciples were facing discouragement. Because of their association with Christ, they became hated objects of the nation Israel. They realized the Jewish leaders would be pleased with Christ's death and that the Jewish populace sought only a political-military Messiah. And instead of seeing Christ rule in kingdom glory and grandeur, the disciples now heard Christ explain "how he must go unto Jerusalem, and suffer many things from the elders and chief priests and scribes, and be killed" (Matt. 16:21).

B. The Persecution of the Disciples

After telling them about His coming death, Christ revealed that the disciples themselves would bear a cross (vv. 24-28). The persecution of God's people is not something new. In the Old Testament God's people were persecuted during both the Egyptian and Babylonian captivities. At times their unique identity as God's people was in danger because of their apostasy and intermarriage with the surrounding nations. There were always times when the train of God's people looked like it was going to come to a halt. And the church, from early days to modern, has experienced severe persecution.

In the midst of the disciples' discouragement Christ assured them that His divine program was moving ahead. He did so by promising to build His church. Although that promise is a brief statement, it provides encouragement for all disciples of Christ. Let's see why.

Lesson

I. THE CERTAINTY OF THE CHURCH'S EXISTENCE

"I will build my church."

It's certain that Christ will build His church because it's His divine promise (cf. Isa. 55:11). Christ is God, and God cannot lie. The tense of the verb emphasizes the continuation of action, not the time of action. That is, Christ has already been building in the past, is building presently, and will continue to build in the future.

A. Because of the Divine Method

Christ is certain to build His church wherever believers live in righteous obedience to God's Word. By walking within the parameters set by Scripture, believers become channels through which Christ builds His church. But Christ will not build where He finds disobedience.

Church leaders are constantly looking for some tricks of the trade to make the church grow. I'm often asked what methods I use. But God doesn't build His church through clever methodology, only through believers committed to righteousness. If you obey God's Word, you'll let Christ build the church His way.

B. Because of the Divine Builder

Scripture clearly shows that Christ is the divine Builder of the church.

1. Acts 2:39—"The promise [of salvation] is unto you, and to your children, and to all that are afar off,

23

even as many as the Lord our God shall call." It is the Lord who calls sinners to repentance.

2. John 6:37—Jesus said, "All that the Father giveth me shall come to me; and him that cometh to me I will in no wise cast out."

3. Acts 2:47—"The Lord added to the church daily such as should be saved."

4. Acts 5:14—"Believers were the more added to the Lord, multitudes both of men and women" (cf. 11:24).

5. Acts 13:48—"When the Gentiles heard this, they were glad, and glorified the Word of the Lord; and as many as were ordained to eternal life believed." God drew to salvation the ones He predetermined to set His love on.

6. Acts 18:10—The Lord said to Paul, "I am with thee, and no man shall set on thee to hurt thee; for I have many people in this city." The Lord brought a select number of believers into His church at Corinth.

The epistles add more detail about how the Lord builds His church. For instance, we are instructed about worship, prayer, teaching, holiness, church discipline, and the qualifications for elders, deacons, and deaconesses. Those instructions point to the need for righteous living, which characterizes those the Lord uses in building His church.

C. Because of the Divine Goal

The church exists to manifest Christ's glory. Ephesians 5 says Christ is building the church to "sanctify and cleanse it with the washing of water by the word; that he might present it to himself a glorious church, not having spot, or wrinkle, or any such thing; but that it should be holy and without blemish" (vv. 26-27). Indeed, "unto Him be glory in the church by Christ Jesus" (Eph. 3:21). Such glory manifests God's infinite wisdom to even the holy angels (3:10).

II. THE INTIMACY BETWEEN CHRIST AND HIS PEOPLE

"I will build *my* church."

The Greek term translated "my" shows Christ to be the Owner, Architect, and Builder of the church. We are part of His own Body and one with Him in holy intimacy (Eph. 5:23). That intimacy is depicted throughout Scripture.

A. In the New Testament

   1. Acts 20:28—"Feed the church of God, which he hath purchased with his own blood."

   2. Acts 9:4—Christ said to Saul, "Why persecutest thou me?" When Saul persecuted Christians, it was the same as persecuting Christ.

   3. 1 Corinthians 6:17—"He that is joined unto the Lord is one spirit."

   4. John 10:27-28—Jesus said, "My sheep hear my voice, and I know them, and they follow me. . . . Neither shall any man pluck them out of my hand."

B. In the Old Testament

   The Old Testament refers to the righteous as the apple of God's eye (Ps. 17:8; Zech. 2:8). That figurative expression refers to the pupil, the most sensitive part of the eye. God was saying, "If you poke your finger in the eyes of My people, it's the same as poking it in My eye." God cares like that because the church has been purchased with Christ's own blood (Acts 20:28). God draws near to His people and is like the friend who sticks closer than a brother (cf. Prov. 18:24).

The Wonder of Intimacy with Christ

As I was returning home on an airplane, a passenger asked me if I drink.

I replied, "I don't drink."

He asked, "Never?"

I said, "Never."

He asked, "Do you have cancer?"

I answered, "As far as I know I don't."

He said, as though he were preaching to me, "I drink every day. Some day you're going to be old and then what are you going to do? All the fun will be behind you. You should drink now while you're still young."

I replied, "I don't have any desire to drink—none at all."

Then he looked at me and asked, "What do you have that you don't need to drink?"

I responded, "I'm glad you asked. I have total peace and happiness."

He asked, "Where did you get that?"
And I answered, "I know Jesus Christ."

There was momentary silence. Then he asked in disbelief, "You know Jesus Christ?"

I said, "That's right. I know Jesus Christ."

He looked at me in bewilderment and remarked, "I went to a school where they told us about Jesus Christ, but I don't know Him."

I responded, "You can." I then had an opportunity to explain the gospel to him.

He went back to his seat, and I took my seat behind him. He then told his traveling partner, "You won't believe this, but the gentleman seated behind us actually knows Jesus Christ!" And his partner, turning around to look at me, said, "You're kidding!" He also was amazed that someone could know Christ personally.

III. THE IDENTITY OF THOSE IN THE CHURCH

"I will build my *church.*"

The Greek term translated "church" (*ekklēsia*) means "called out ones" and refers to an assembly. In the gospels the word occurs only here and in Matthew 18:17. Here it is used in its general sense for any gathering of people. The original meaning of the word *synagogue* also referred to a general gathering of people. Since it is likely Christ spoke in Aramaic, He probably used the general term *kahal*, which means "congregation," "assembly," or "multitude." Only later in the epistles do we find *ekklēsia* invested with a fuller meaning. So Christ was speaking of an assembly, congregation, or community of redeemed people. That general meaning is also evident in other Scriptures.

A. Acts 7:37-38—"This is that Moses who said unto the children of Israel, A Prophet shall the Lord your God raise up unto you of your brethren, like me; him shall ye hear. This is he that was in the church in the wilderness with the angel who spoke to him in Mount Sinai." Here the word refers to the Jewish people gathered in the desert during the time of Moses.

B. Acts 19:32—"Some, therefore, cried one thing, and some another; for the assembly was in confusion." Here *ekklēsia* refers to a crowd in Ephesus that rejected the gospel message.

C. Hebrews 12:22-23—"Ye are come unto Mount Zion, and unto the city of the living God, the heavenly Jerusalem, and to an innumerable company of angels, to the general assembly and church of the first-born, who are written in heaven, and to God, the Judge of all and to the spirits of just men made perfect." Here "church" refers to all God's people.

Just as in Hebrews 12:23, "church" in Matthew 16 refers to all God's people. And "kingdom of heaven" in Matthew 16:19—used synonymously for the word *church*—also speaks of the assembly of people gathered to God. As the disciples were walking along the dusty road in Caesarea Philippi, they certainly understood *ekklēsia* in the same general sense, not as a building with a steeple. In those days there were no denominations, elders, deacons, or congregations as we have today. Although Christ was facing hostility and rejection, He would continue to gather His redeemed people, just as He had been doing all along and is continuing to do now.

Conclusion

People often wonder what will happen to the church if America falls. But the building of the church doesn't depend on the rise or fall of America because only the Lord builds the church. Since Christ builds only where He finds righteousness, it's important for us to live righteously. Be committed to His Word and allow His Spirit to change your life. That way you'll manifest His glory in the church.

Focusing on the Facts

1. What statement is the heart of Matthew 16:13-20 (see p. 21)?
2. It's a _____ for the believer to be a part of what God is building (see p. 22).
3. Why were Christ's disciples discouraged (see p. 22)?
4. What is the significance of the verb tense in Matthew 16:18 (see p. 23)?
5. Where is Christ certain to build His church (see p. 23)?
6. Christ builds His church through believers committed to _____(see p. 23).
7. What does Acts 2:39 show (see pp. 23-24)?
8. The _____ add more detail about how the Lord builds His church (see p. 24).
9. Why does the church exist (see p. 24)?

10. The term "my" in Matthew 16:18 reveals the believer to be _____ with Christ in holy _____ (see p. 25).
11. In Acts 9:4 who in effect is Saul persecuting (see p. 25)?
12. Why did the Lord call His people "the apple of his eye" (Zech. 2:8; see p. 25)?
13. Define "church" in Matthew 16:18. Support your answer with Scripture (see p. 27).

Pondering the Principles

1. As part of the church Christians enjoy holy intimacy with Christ. Bible scholar R. B. Kuiper wrote, "How the Creator can regard mere creatures as His friends defies human understanding. How the holy God can bestow His friendship on sinful men is utterly incomprehensible. Suffice it to say that here we witness a supreme manifestation of divine condescension. And the intimacy of that friendship renders the divine condescension all the more marvelous" (*The Glorious Body of Christ* [Edinburgh: The Banner of Truth Trust, 1967], pp. 332-33). Are you enjoying intimacy with the Lord through the study of His Word and prayer? Read and study Luke 10:38-42, examining your walk with the Lord in light of that Scripture. Ask the Lord to help you have the same desire the apostle Paul had: "I count all things to be loss in view of the surpassing value of knowing Christ Jesus my Lord, for whom I have suffered the loss of all things, and count them but rubbish in order that I may gain Christ" (Phil. 3:8, NASB*).

2. Nothing can thwart Christ's promise to build His church. Pastor-teacher J. C. Ryle said, "Great is the power which Christ displays in building His church! He carries on His work in spite of opposition from the world, the flesh and the devil. In storm, in tempest, through troublous times, silently, quietly, without noise, without stir, without excitement, the building progresses. . . . We ought to feel deeply thankful that the building of the true church is laid on the shoulders of One that is mighty. If the work depended on man, it would

---

* *New American Standard Bible.*

soon stand still. But, blessed be God, the work is in the hands of a Builder who never fails to accomplish His designs! Christ is the almighty Builder. He will carry on His work, though nations and visible churches may not know their duty. Christ will never fail. That which He has undertaken He will certainly accomplish" (*Holiness* [Hertfordshire, England: Evangelical Press, 1989], p. 214). Have you offered thanks and praise to the Lord for building His church? Read Ephesians 1 and worship the Lord for His marvelous work.

3
The Church That Christ Builds—Part 2

Outline

Introduction
A. A Look at Life
   1. From the perspective of the lost
   2. From the perspective of Scripture
B. A Look at the Disciples
   1. Their expectations
   2. Their perplexity

Review
I. The Certainty of the Church's Existence (v. 18)
II. The Intimacy Between Christ and His People (v. 18)
III. The Identity of Those in the Church (v. 18)

Lesson
IV. The Foundation of the Church (v. 18)
A. Is It Peter?
B. Is It Peter's Confession?
C. Is It the Apostles?
V. The Invincibility of the Church (v. 18)
VI. The Authority of All Believers (v. 19)
A. Based on God's Word
B. Exercised in the Church
VII. The Spirituality of the Church (v. 20)

Introduction

A. A Look at Life

   1. From the perspective of the lost

Throughout history philosophers and historians have wondered why man exists. For instance, the modern French author André Maurois wrote a book on the subject entitled *Relativism*. He believed the universe was indifferent, concluding there is no way for anyone to attain total, absolute truth in any area. Several ancient Greek philosophers had a similar view, seeing life as a constant repetition of cycles without any purpose or goal. The popular French writer Jean-Paul Sartre espoused the view that every person exists as an isolated individual in the midst of a purposeless universe. The French molecular biologist Jacques Monod wrote that man exists because of chance and lives without duty or destiny (*Chance and Necessity* [New York: Alfred A. Knopf, 1971]). With that kind of philosophy being espoused, is it any wonder that people have reached the point of despair and our society is filled with violence, destruction, and hedonism?

   2. From the perspective of Scripture

According to Scripture, man exists to glorify God. That's why the Bible says we are to "confess that Jesus Christ is Lord, to the glory of God" (Phil. 2:11). And "whatever ye do, do all to the glory of God" (1 Cor. 10:31). God alone is worthy to receive glory and has created man to reflect His eternal majesty and splendor. To that end, God is saving a redeemed people out of a sinful world.

B. A Look at the Disciples

   1. Their expectations

In Matthew 16 Christ wanted to assure His disciples that the unfolding of history would continue to bring Him glory. They were anticipating the Messiah to come and reign as King, delivering the Jewish people from bondage and oppression, while ushering in righteousness, peace, and prosperity. Tragically, the Jewish populace didn't even recognize their Messiah. They thought He was John the Baptist, Elijah, Jeremiah, or one of the other prophets. Besides that, the Jewish religious leaders hated Christ and wanted Him killed. So the disciples' expectations for a conquering king appeared unfulfilled.

Their level of anticipation certainly didn't rise any when Christ said "he must go unto Jerusalem, and suffer many things . . . and be killed" (Matt. 16:21). In fact, their feelings were so to the contrary that Peter blurted out, "Be it far from thee, Lord; this shall not be unto thee" (v. 22). Christ replied, "If any man will come after me, let him deny himself, and take up his cross, and follow me. For whosoever will save his life shall lose it; and whosoever will lose his life for my sake shall find it" (vv. 24-25). Death would come not only to Christ, but also to the disciples. But in spite of such gloom, the disciples confessed, "Thou art the Christ, the son of the living God" (v. 16).

2. Their perplexity

Although the disciples collectively made that confession, they were still perplexed about the unfolding of the messianic kingdom. What had happened to it? Was it still on schedule? In response to what they must have been thinking, Christ promised, "I will [continue to] build my church, and the gates of [death] shall not prevail against it" (v. 18). Undoubtedly that promise brought the disciples confidence and encouragement.

Whenever you wonder if history is ultimately bringing glory to God, find your assurance and strength in those same words. In history God is calling an assembly of redeemed people to the eternal praise of

His glory. Let's continue our study of that divine assembly called the church.

Review

I. THE CERTAINTY OF THE CHURCH'S EXISTENCE (v. 18; see pp. 23-24)

II. THE INTIMACY BETWEEN CHRIST AND HIS PEOPLE (v. 18; see pp. 25-27)

III. THE IDENTITY OF THOSE IN THE CHURCH (v. 18; see pp. 27-28)

Lesson

IV. THE FOUNDATION OF THE CHURCH (v. 18)

"Thou art Peter, and upon this rock I will build my church."

"This rock" identifies the foundation on which the church is built. There are several views about the identity of that foundation. Some say it is the apostle Peter, some say it is Peter's confession, and others say it is all the apostles.

A. Is It Peter?

Many believe the church is built on the apostle Peter—that he is the father or first head of the church. This is the traditional view of the Roman Catholic church. Its advocates point out that the Greek name "Peter" means "rock" or "stone." They teach that Peter's authority passed from him to a successor bearing the same authority. They consider that authority to be as binding as the Bible.

However, Scripture clearly reveals that Christ, not Peter, is the head of the church (Eph. 5:23). In Matthew 18 the disciples come to Jesus asking, "Who is the greatest in the kingdom of heaven?" (v. 1). If it were obvious to them that Peter was the greatest, there would have been no need to ask. Therefore the keys of the kingdom mentioned two chapters previously (Matt. 16:19) must not have belonged to Peter alone. In comparing greatness to the humility of a little child (18:4), Christ didn't reveal any kingdom primacy for Peter.

In Matthew 20:21 we find a similar incident. The mother of James and John asked Christ to allow her two sons to sit next to Him in His kingdom. That's another clear indication that neither James nor John knew of any kingdom primacy that had been given to Peter. Otherwise there would have been no need for the mother's question.

Did Peter himself think he was the father or head of the church? In his first epistle he wrote, "The elders who are among you I exhort, who am *also* an elder" (1 Peter 5:1, emphasis added). Peter recognized the elders in the church as his equals and addressed them as such. He knew it was important for elders not to abuse their authority, but instead to "be clothed with humility" (v. 5).

B. Is It Peter's Confession?

The traditional Protestant view is that "this rock" refers to Peter's confession: "Thou art the Christ, the Son of the living God" (Matt. 16:16). The Greek name translated "Peter" (*petros*) means "rock," but "this rock" (*petra*, a different form of the same basic word) refers to a larger rock such as a rock bed or a rocky mountain or peak. That leads some to believe the antecedent of "this rock" is Peter's confession—that Christ was saying He would build His church on the rock bed of Peter's confession about the reality of Christ's deity. That's a fair interpretation because there is a distinction in meaning between the two words.

C. Is It the Apostles?

I believe, however, that the best interpretation of "upon this rock I will build my church" is to see the apostles as the foundation of the church. Ephesians 2 says the household of God (the church) is "built upon the foundation of the apostles and prophets, Jesus Christ himself being the chief corner stone" (v. 20). It's important to remember that Peter made his confession about Christ (Matt. 16:16) on behalf of all the disciples. So it's no problem to see Peter representing all the disciples here in verse 18.

This isn't the only occasion where Peter served as spokesman for the twelve (e.g., Matt. 15:15; 19:27; John 6:68). Furthermore, he had a leading role in ministering on behalf all the disciples in the days of the early church. For example, the Lord used his preaching to add more than five thousand people to the church (Acts 4:4). It was through Peter's testimony and ministry that a lame man was healed (3:4-6). Peter had a leading part in guiding the election process for a replacement for Judas (1:15-22). And before the Sanhedrin Peter heroically proclaimed Jesus Christ (4:8-12).

The church is built, not on the office or rank of the apostles, but on their teaching. The apostles laid the foundation for the church in proclaiming the Word of God and in many ways were inseparable from their own message. Acts 2 says the early church "continued steadfastly in the apostles' doctrine and fellowship" (v. 42). The church's foundation is God's revelation, as given to us through the apostles.

In 1 Corinthians 3:11 Paul says, "No man can lay a foundation other than the one which is laid, which is Jesus Christ" (NASB). That complements what he wrote in Ephesians 2:20: the apostles and prophets were chosen to be foundation stones because they confessed Christ to be the true foundation. They were intimately attached and inseparably linked to Christ and His Word. Saying the church is built on the foundation of the apostles is the same as saying that it's built on Christ. And today

Christ is still building His church on people who, like the apostles, embrace Christ as Lord.

V. THE INVINCIBILITY OF THE CHURCH (v. 18)

"The gates of hades shall not prevail against it."

"Gates" is used here in the sense of holding people in—like prison gates. "Hades" is the New Testament equivalent of the Old Testament term "sheol." It's a general reference to the grave, not to the eternal torments of hell. The Greek term translated "prevail" means "to conquer." According to Hebrews 2:14 Satan has the power of death, so he tries to kill Christians in an attempt to destroy the church. But he will never prevail because "God hath raised up [Christ], having loosed the pains of death, because it was not possible that he should be held by it" (Acts 2:24).

Because death could not hold Christ captive, the believer is also set free from death's bondage. Christ said it like this: "Because I live, ye shall live also" (John 14:19). First Corinthians 15 says, "O death, where is thy sting? O grave, where is thy victory? . . . But thanks be to God, who giveth us the victory through our Lord Jesus Christ" (vv. 55, 57).

So Christ's statement in Matthew 16:18 is a promise of resurrection. That certainly fits the context of the passage because Christ would soon tell them not only about His death and resurrection (v. 21), but also about the coming persecution and death of His followers (v. 25). Death won't defeat Christ's program of building the church. Everyone who loves Christ leaves this world to enter into God's glorious world "to the general assembly and church of the first-born who are enrolled in heaven" (Heb. 12:23, NASB). Christ said, "I am he that liveth, and was dead; and, behold, I am alive for evermore, Amen, and have the keys of hades and of death" (Rev. 1:18). Christ has complete authority and control over death. He experienced death so "he might destroy him that had the power of death, that is, the devil" (Heb. 2:14).

"I will give unto thee the keys of the kingdom of heaven; and whatsoever thou shalt bind on earth shall be bound in heaven; and whatsoever thou shalt loose on earth shall be loosed in heaven."

Here Christ was giving the disciples authority to approve (bind) or disapprove (loose) the actions of others. Christ spoke of that same authority in John 20:23: "Whosoever's sins ye remit, they are remitted unto them; and whosoever's sins ye retain, they are retained." In Matthew 18:18 Christ gave the entire church that authority by saying, "Whatsoever ye shall bind on earth shall be bound in heaven; and whatsoever ye shall loose on earth shall be loosed in heaven." So the kind of authority Christ spoke about in Matthew 16 was given not only to Peter and the other apostles, but also to every believer.

A. Based on God's Word

All believers have that authority because God's Word reveals to us the kind of behavior God approves or disapproves of. So if you ask a man if he has received Christ as his Lord and Savior and he says yes, you can say, "Your sins are forgiven." But if he says no you can say, "Your sins aren't forgiven." Similarly, we can say to others, "It's wrong to do that." If what we say is based on God's Word—not on a person's title, office, human worthiness, or intelligence—we know it will concur with what's said in heaven. Because God's Word is our authority, it's important that we not compromise the truth it teaches.

B. Exercised in the Church

God has entrusted the Word to His church so that it might shine as a light in the world (Matt. 5:14). When the church upholds the Word, the Lord's will is done on earth as it is in heaven (Matt. 6:9). That way the church serves as a divine pattern for the lost world to see. It has a responsibility to tell the lost about sin, righteousness, and judgment. By our telling them what God's Word says, they will hear what heaven says.

Because God has given His Word to the church, the church is His authority in the world. With such divine authority, there's no need to worry about the world's reaction to the gospel message. Even though many will reject Christ, the church must never compromise the truth. Upholding the standard of His Word will bring Him the glory He deserves.

VII. THE SPIRITUALITY OF THE CHURCH (v. 20)

"Then charged he his disciples that they should tell no man that he was Jesus, the Christ."

Because most Jewish people were expecting the Messiah to be a political and military figure, Christ knew their hearing He was the Messiah would only add to their hatred of Him (cf. Matt. 7:6). He was reminding His disciples that the church is a spiritual entity, not a political or military kingdom. Later He told them to "wait for the promise of the Father" (Acts 1:4)—the promise of receiving power from the Holy Spirit to witness about Christ "in Jerusalem, and in all Judaea, and in Samaria, and unto the uttermost part of the earth" (v. 8; cf. Mark 16:15). When that promise was fulfilled on the Day of Pentecost, the disciples' witness became bold and clear: "Let all the house of Israel know assuredly, that God hath made that same Jesus, whom ye have crucified, both Lord and Christ" (Acts 2:36).

Focusing on the Facts

1. Summarize how the lost look at life (see p. 32).
2. According to Scripture, why does man exist (1 Cor. 10:31; see p. 32)?
3. In what way did the disciples anticipate the Messiah's coming? What happened to their level of anticipation (see pp. 32-33)?
4. What caused the disciples to be perplexed? How did Christ respond to them (see pp. 33-34)?

5. "_____" identifies the foundation on which the church is built (Matt. 16:18; see p. 34).

6. Why is it not correct to say that the church is built on Peter alone? Support your answer with Scripture (see pp. 34-35).

7. Explain the traditional Protestant view of "this rock" (v. 18; see p. 35).

8. Perhaps the most biblical view is to see the _____ as the foundation of the church (see p. 36).

9. Today what kind of people is Christ building His church on (see p. 37)?

10. What does "hades" refer to in Matthew 16:18 (see p. 37)?

11. In what way is Satan's activity against the church limited (see p. 37)?

12. "The gates of hades shall not prevail against it" (Matt. 16:18) is a promise of _____ (see p. 37).

13. If what we say is based on God's Word, what will it concur with (see p. 38)?

Pondering the Principles

1. London pastor Samuel J. Stone's hymn "The Church's One Foundation" is based on the Apostles' Creed and affirms Christ as Lord and foundation of the church. Read through it slowly and meditatively, allowing it to deepen your love for Christ and His church:

   The Church's one foundation is Jesus Christ her Lord;
   She is His new creation by water and the word:
   From Heav'n He came and sought her to be His holy bride;
   With His own blood He bought her, and for her life He
       died.

   Elect from ev'ry nation, yet one o'er all the earth,
   Her charter of salvation, one Lord, one faith, one birth;
   One holy name she blesses, partakes one holy food,
   And to one hope she presses, with ev'ry grace endued.

   Though with a scornful wonder men see her sore op-
       pressed,
   By schisms rent asunder, by heresies distressed.

Yet saints their watch are keeping, their cry goes up,
"How long?"
And soon the night of weeping shall be the morn of song.

'Mid toil and tribulation, and tumult of her war,
She waits the consummation of peace forevermore;
Till, with the vision glorious, her longing eyes are blest,
And the great church victorious shall be the church at
rest.

2. God's Word is the basis of the church's authority. In his
    Body of Divinity Puritan Thomas Watson wrote, "The Word of
    God, which is contained in the scriptures of the Old and
    New Testaments, is the only rule to direct us how we may
    glorify and enjoy him. . . . The Word is a rule of faith, a
    canon to direct our lives. The Word is the judge of contro-
    versies, the rock of infallibility. That only is to be received
    for truth which agrees with Scripture. . . . All maxims in di-
    vinity are to be brought to the touchstone of Scripture, as
    all measures are brought to the standard" ([Edinburgh:
    Banner of Truth Trust, 1986], pp. 26, 30). Since God's Word
    is vital to the church, it's important for you to be a serious
    student of it. One way to study is through reading liter-
    ature and listening to messages that explain the meaning of
    Scripture. Make it your priority to be a student of the
    Word!

4
Offending Christ

Outline

Introduction

Review

Lesson
I. The Plan of God (v. 21)
   A. Its Unveiling (v. 21a)
   B. Its Necessity (v. 21b)
   C. Its Content (v. 21c)
      1. Christ's journey to Jerusalem
      2. Christ's suffering
      3. Christ's death
      4. Christ's resurrection
II. The Presumption of Peter (v. 22)
   A. He Took Christ Aside (v. 22a)
   B. He Rebuked Christ (v. 22b)
III. The Protest of Christ (v. 23a-b)
   A. Against Satan (v. 23a)
   B. Against Peter (v. 23b)
IV. The Principle for Us (v. 23c)

Conclusion

Introduction

Our study of the church concludes in Matthew 16:21-23: "From that time forth began Jesus to show unto his disciples how he must go unto Jerusalem, and suffer many things from the elders and chief priests and scribes, and be killed, and be raised again the third day. Then Peter took him, and began to rebuke him, saying, Be it far from thee, Lord; this shall not be unto thee. But he turned and said unto Peter, Get thee behind me, Satan. Thou art an offense unto me; for thou savorest not the things that are of God, but those that are of men."

Throughout its pages the Bible emphasizes how man sees things one way, but God sees them another. For example, Proverbs 14:12 says, "There is a way which seemeth right unto a man, but the end thereof are the ways of death." Psalm 77:19 points out that God's footsteps are not known to man. Psalm 92 says, "O Lord, how great are thy works! And thy thoughts are very deep. A [senseless] man knoweth not, neither doth a fool understand this" (vv. 5-6).

By trusting in our human understanding alone, we will miss what God is doing in our lives. Peter was like that. In his human wisdom he tried to correct the Lord. We also try to correct the Lord when things don't go our way. Like Peter we savor our way instead of God's. So we should seek to see things the way God does. That's what Christ taught the disciples in this passage.

Now the disciples acknowledged Christ to be the Messiah, but they didn't understand that He had to suffer and die. In a sense they were thinking like the lost because "the cross is to them that perish foolishness" (1 Cor. 1:18). Their understanding was so incomplete that Christ ordered "his disciples that they should tell no man that he was Jesus, the Christ" (Matt. 16:20).

From the disciples' vantage point, the Messiah was destined to reign in glory, not suffer in humiliation. Their view was especially evident when Jesus stooped to wash their feet. Peter told the Lord, "Thou shalt never wash my feet" (John 13:8). It didn't seem right to Peter that the Messiah should serve others. And when Christ was arrested just prior to His crucifixion, "all the disciples forsook him, and fled" (Matt. 26:56). Even after Christ's death, the disciples continued to be confused about what happened (Mark 16:12-13).

44

In Matthew 16:21-23 we read of Christ's beginning to instruct the disciples about His coming humiliation, death, and resurrection. But the disciples' response to Christ's instruction greatly offended Him. To understand why, we need to look closely at what both Christ and His disciples were saying that day.

Review

On behalf of all the disciples Peter confessed Christ to be the Messiah (v. 16; see pp. 10-11). For more than two years they heard His teaching and saw His supernatural works. Revelation from God, not human wisdom, led them to their great confession of faith (v. 17; see pp. 12-16).

Although most Jewish people were expecting the Messiah to be a political and military figure, Christ came to build a spiritual entity called the church. Not even death itself can defeat His mission (v. 18; see pp. 21-28). The church was built on the foundation of the apostles, who confessed Christ to be the true foundation of the church (v. 18; see pp. 34-37). For the time being, however, Christ told His disciples not to confess Him before others until receiving further instruction (v. 20; see p. 39).

Lesson

I. THE PLAN OF GOD (v. 21)

"From that time forth began Jesus to show unto his disciples, how he must go unto Jerusalem, and suffer many things from the elders and chief priests and scribes, and be killed, and be raised again the third day."

A. Its Unveiling (v. 21a)

"From that time forth began Jesus to show unto his disciples."

The Greek phrase translated "from that time forth" marks a key transition in the book of Matthew. In

Matthew 4:17 that same phrase signifies the beginning of Christ's public ministry to Israel. Here it denotes the beginning of Christ's private ministry to His disciples. Christ "began" the process of showing His disciples that He must die and be raised from the dead.

B. Its Necessity (v. 21b)

"How he must."

The Greek term translated "must" reveals the divine necessity for Christ's death and resurrection. His atoning work was set in motion before the foundation of the world and made necessary by four things. First, it was necessary because of human need. Man is a sinner and cannot have eternal life unless his sins are paid for (Rom. 5:6-8). Second, it was necessary because of the redemptive requirement. Hebrews 9:22 says there is no remission for sins without the shedding of blood (physical death). Third, it was necessary because of divine decree. By God's determinant counsel and foreknowledge, He brought Christ's death and resurrection to pass (Acts 2:23). Fourth, it was necessary to fulfill the prophetic promises foretelling the Messiah's death (Matt. 26:53-54; Luke 24:25-26).

There are no alternatives or options to God's eternal and sovereign plans. No one has the right to say, "Lord, I have a better plan, and I'd like You to change your plans." That may sound ridiculous, yet we can be tempted to think that way when difficult circumstances arise.

C. Its Content (v. 21c)

"Go unto Jerusalem, and suffer many things from the elders and chief priests and scribes, and be killed, and be raised again the third day."

1. Christ's journey to Jerusalem

It was necessary for Christ to "go unto Jerusalem," the city of sacrifices, to be the Passover Lamb (1 Cor. 5:7). Presently He was secluded in safety with His disciples in Caesarea Philippi, but His arrival in Jerusalem would expose Him to great opposition and danger. That's why Thomas said to the other disciples, "Let us also go [to Jerusalem], that we may die with him" (John 11:16). The Jewish religious leaders of Jerusalem instigated most of the trouble against Christ (cf. Matt. 15:1-2). Because the Lord exposed their hypocritical self righteousness and self-centeredness, they hated Him.

But Christ willingly offered Himself to His enemies. He said, "I lay down my life, that I might take it again. No man taketh it from me, but I lay it down of myself. I have power to lay it down, and I have power to take it again" (John 10:17-18). Just prior to His crucifixion Christ told the Roman procurator Pontius Pilate, "Thou couldest have no power at all against me, except it were given thee from above" (John 19:11; cf. Matt. 26:53).

Receiving Back Jerusalem

Jerusalem means "foundation of peace." The city is about thirty miles east of the Mediterranean Sea, ten miles west of the Dead Sea, and elevated on a plateau about twenty-five hundred feet above sea level. Its highest point is the Mount of Olives. Because it sparkles in the sun, the city is also known as the Golden City.

We are first introduced to it in Genesis 14:18, when it was then called Salem and administered by Melchizedek, who is a picture of Christ. The Jerusalem area includes Mount Moriah, the place where Abraham went to sacrifice his son Isaac. There the Lord provided a sacrificial animal—another picture of Christ—to take Isaac's place. Later, David captured it from the Jebusites, naming it the City of David and making it the capital of Israel (2 Sam. 5:5-9). Later he brought the Ark of the Covenant (the symbolic place of God's dwelling) there, and eventually it became known as the City of God (Ps. 87:3). King Solomon, describing the city as "comely" (Song of Sol. 6:4), built the Temple there (2 Chron. 3:1).

Jerusalem was the sacred center of worship for the Jewish people. In both prosperity and destruction it remained the city of God in the hearts of its people. The psalmist expressed it this way: "If I forget thee, O Jerusalem, let my right hand forget.her cunning. If I do not remember thee, let my tongue cleave to the roof of my mouth, if I prefer not Jerusalem above my chief joy" (Ps. 137:5-6). Back then the Jewish people loved the city, and today they still do.

In practice, however, Jerusalem was neither the city of God nor the foundation of peace. In the days of Christ the city was in fact extremely hostile to God. King Herod sought to kill Christ as an infant (Matt. 2:13). Christ was hated for cleansing the defiled Temple (Matt. 21:12-15) and healing a lame man on the Sabbath (John 5:16). Later in the year He attended the Feast of Tabernacles, and the religious leaders tried to arrest Him (John 7:32). In John 8 the people tried to stone Him for teaching in the Temple (v. 59). When He taught there again from Solomon's porch, He had to escape for His life (10:39). And when He later returned for His last Passover, He was killed.

It's not difficult to see why Jerusalem received a new name, given in Revelation 11:8: "Their dead bodies shall lie in the street of the great city, which is spiritually called Sodom and Egypt, where also our Lord was crucified." Jerusalem, however, will receive back its rightful name and be a true foundation of peace when Christ returns to establish His Kingdom (cf. Zech. 14).

2. Christ's suffering

In addition to going to Jerusalem it was also necessary for Christ to "suffer many things from the elders and chief priests and scribes" (Matt. 16:21). Those three groups constituted the Sanhedrin, which was the legal court in Israel. Elders were respected tribal heads who became leaders and judges throughout the land. The chief priests were primarily Sadducees, and the scribes were primarily Pharisees. They were the religious leaders of Israel who placed Christ on trial. In truth His trial was a mockery, but from their viewpoint it stood as a formal trial and condemnation.

3. Christ's death

It was necessary for Christ to "be killed," a Greek term that means "to be murdered," "be robbed of life," or "put away." The term carries no thought of just punishment for a crime. In a veiled way the disciples previously heard Christ tell of His death when He said, "Destroy this temple, and in three days I will raise it up" (John 2:19). John the Baptist said it this way: "Behold the Lamb of God, who taketh away the sin of the world" (1:29). But here in Matthew 16:21 Christ's statement about His death is so explicit that the disciples finally understand He is telling them He will die. It grabbed their attention in such a way that they seemed not to have heard what He said next about His resurrection.

4. Christ's resurrection

Christ plainly stated it was necessary that He "be raised again the third day." Earlier He made this veiled statement to the scribes and Pharisees about His resurrection: "As Jonah was three days and three nights in the belly of the great fish, so shall the Son of man be three days and three nights in the heart of the earth" (Matt. 12:40). Perhaps He was specific about the three days because He didn't want the disciples to be thinking like Martha, who said about her brother Lazarus, "I know that he shall rise again in the resurrection at the last day" (John 11:24). Christ's unique resurrection would occur within three days, not at the last day near the end of time.

Even though Christ's statement was explicit, the disciples didn't fully grasp what He said. They knew Christ had raised Jairus's daughter (Mark 5:22-24, 35-42) and the widow's son in the village of Nain (Luke 7:11-16). But maybe they were thinking, If Christ Himself is killed, who would raise Him? Perhaps they envisioned the scenario of being left with a dead Messiah. Whatever their reasoning, Peter took the opportunity to object to what Christ said. Peter's brashness is especially shocking when considering that Christ just said the gates of death would not conquer His kingdom program of building the church.

II. THE PRESUMPTION OF PETER (v. 22)

"Then Peter took him, and began to rebuke him, saying, Be it far from thee, Lord; this shall not be unto thee."

A. He Took Christ Aside (v. 22*a*)

"Then Peter took him."

Peter took Christ aside to straighten out His supposedly wrong thinking. The Greek term "took" suggests that Peter caught hold of Him and forced Him aside. Peter's action accentuates not only his brashness, but also Christ's humanity. Because God condescended to reveal Himself in the flesh through Christ, Peter could talk to Him as a man talks to his friend.

Although Peter's reaction was presumptuous, you and I can respond in a similar way. In the midst of difficult circumstances have you ever said, "I don't understand why I must go through this trial and suffer so"? Perhaps the trial is the loss of a loved one or a job. Whatever it is, it's tempting to offer God an alternative plan that would eliminate the difficulty. Often our plan is to have unmitigated joy and bliss, not pain or suffering. But we must ask for the Lord's help in submitting our will to His for what's best in the long run.

B. He Rebuked Christ (v. 22*b*)

"[Peter] began to rebuke him, saying, Be it far from thee, Lord; this shall not be unto thee."

The Greek term translated "rebuke" shows Peter's words to be full of vehemence. He came on strong in his zeal to correct the Lord. Perhaps he did so because of his intimate friendship with Christ. As a disciple Peter had spent much time with Him, and Christ had just said to him, "Blessed art thou. . . . Flesh and blood hath not revealed it unto thee, but my Father" (v. 17). Perhaps feeling a little proud over his friendship with Christ, Peter thought he was more privileged than the others. Whatever the reason, Peter wanted to lead Christ to a better understanding about the meaning of His messiahship.

Peter's plan was for the Messiah to rule in power, glory, pomp, and majesty. But God's eternal plan was for Christ first to suffer, die, and rise from the dead. Because of that difference, Peter said to Christ, "Be it far from thee," an idiom that means "Pity thyself," "God be gracious to you," or "Heaven forbid." Today we would say something like "Give yourself a break" or "Don't be so hard on yourself." Peter addressed Christ as "Lord," but was telling Him what to do. Peter then added, "This shall not be unto thee." That was a bold flat-out rebuke!

III. THE PROTEST OF CHRIST (v. 23a-b)

"But [Christ] turned and said unto Peter, Get thee behind me, Satan. Thou art an offense unto me."

Undoubtedly Christ's reply was a shock to Peter. On the surface Peter's rebuke seemed noble because he didn't want Christ to suffer such horrible pain and death. But God's plan wasn't the same as Peter's, so Christ had to respond to what he said.

A. Against Satan (v. 23a)

"Get thee behind me, Satan."

The Greek phrase translated "get thee behind" means "be gone" or "go away." Verse 22 tells us Peter was just beginning to rebuke Christ. Here we see Christ putting a quick end to it. He knew exactly what was happening—Satan was using the words of Peter to tempt Christ. Satan's approach was similar to the one he used against Christ in the wilderness: trying to entice Him to avoid the cross (Luke 4:4-13). But Christ knew it was the cross where He would bear all the sins of the world. After the temptation in the wilderness, the devil departed from Christ, but only for a season (v. 13). He kept coming back, trying to divert Him from the cross. The heaviness of heart Christ experienced in anticipating the cross was clearly evident in the Garden of Gethsemane. There Christ prayed, "If thou be willing, remove this cup from me. . . . And being in an agony, he prayed more earnestly; and his sweat was, as it were, great drops of blood falling down to the ground" (Luke 22:42, 44). Satan knew the cross would crush his head (Gen. 3:15; cf. Rom. 16:20) and destroy his hold on the power of death (Heb. 2:14). He also knew the cross was where sins would be paid for and where sinners would be liberated from his dark dominion into the kingdom of light. So Satan hated the cross.

B. Against Peter (v. 23*b*)

"Thou art an offense unto me."

Those words were directed against Peter. His presumptuous remarks made him a trap and stumbling block to Christ. The Greek term translated "offense" (*skandalon*) speaks of enticing someone to his doom. The enticement—like a baited trap—was meant to end in another's ruin and destruction. So Christ recognized Peter's words about the cross as a satanic trap. Unfortunately the cross continues to be a stumbling block to most people (1 Cor. 1:23).

Peter didn't realize that his attempt to dissuade Christ from the cross was like putting arrows in Satan's bow to shoot at the Savior. Satan is so subtle: In Peter's desire to love and protect the Lord, he was actually taking Satan's side.

IV. THE PRINCIPLE FOR US (v. 23*c*)

"Thou savorest not the things that are of God, but those that are of men."

The Greek term translated "savorest" (*phroneō*) means "to think." Christ placed Peter's action into a category we all

52

are in from time to time: we sometimes think man's thoughts instead of God's. It was God's eternal plan that His Son should suffer and die. According to man's thinking that plan seems incomprehensible. However, God's ways are not the same as man's (Isa. 55:8). Romans 8 says, "The mind set on the flesh is hostile toward God" (v. 7, NASB). Peter saw only the crucifixion, but not the exaltation. At times we think the same way. Pain is so unpleasant we are prone to see only the present suffering but not the spiritual benefit it accrues (cf. 1 Pet. 1:6-7). We seek to escape the very trials God uses to perfect and conform us to Christ's image (Rom. 8:26-29; James 1:4).

Conclusion

From Christ's words we can learn two main lessons. The first is that Christ is the Messiah, the fulfillment of God's redemptive plan, but to seek the Messiah apart from His death, burial, and resurrection is to set oneself against God. Peter later understood that and wrote, "Blessed be the God and Father of our Lord Jesus Christ, who, according to his abundant mercy, hath begotten us again unto a living hope by the resurrection of Jesus Christ from the dead" (1 Pet. 1:3; cf. vv. 18-21).

The second lesson is that God refines us through suffering. To follow Christ means we take up a cross and lose our life in the process (Matt. 16:24-25). There are no crowns without thorns. God refines us like gold, burning off the dross of sin to make us spiritually pure. So when trials come, we should pray, "Lord, help me to accept Your will as my will." That became Peter's prayer for us all: "The God of all grace, who hath called us unto his eternal glory by Christ Jesus, after ye have suffered awhile, make you perfect, establish, strengthen, settle you. To him be glory and dominion forever and ever" (1 Pet. 5:10-11).

Focusing on the Facts

1. What didn't the disciples fully grasp about the Messiah (see pp. 42-43)?

2. What is the significance of "from that time forth" in Matthew 16:21 (see pp. 45-46)?

3. What four things made Christ's death and resurrection necessary? Support your answer with Scripture (see p. 46).

4. What does the disciple Thomas's comment about Jerusalem imply about Christ's status there (John 11:16; see p. 47)?

5. What city in Israel is called "Sodom" and "Egypt" (Rev. 11:8)? Why (see p. 48)?

6. Who were the "elders and chief priests and scribes" (Matt. 16:21; see p. 48)?

7. What is the meaning of the Greek term translated "be killed" in Matthew 16:21 (see p. 49)?

8. Once the disciples understood Christ was telling them He would be killed, they seemingly never heard His next words about the _____ (see p. 49).

9. What does "took" suggest in Matthew 16:22 (see p. 50)?

10. We must ask for the Lord's help in submitting our will to _____ (see p. 50).

11. What was Peter's purpose in rebuking Christ (see pp. 50-51)?

12. In what specific way was Satan tempting Christ? How do we know it must have been a weighty temptation? Support your answer with Scripture (see pp. 51-52).

13. What is the significance of "offense" in Matthew 16:23 (see p. 52)?

14. The _____ remains a stumbling block to many people (1 Cor. 1:23; see p. 52).

15. What does God use to perfect and conform us to Christ's image (James 1:4; see p. 53)?

16. What are two main lessons we can learn from Matthew 16:21-23 (see p. 53)?

Pondering the Principles

1. As Christ was coming to the crucial point of fulfilling God's eternal redemptive plan on the cross, Peter gave wrong counsel to the Lord. Peter's seeming benevolence contradicted God's revealed will. When counseling others, be certain your words reflect the truths of Scripture. When receiving counsel, make sure you check the advice against God's Word. Pay close attention to what the following Scriptures say about good and bad counsel:

- Exodus 18:13-25—Why did the people come to Moses (v. 15)? What was Moses to tell the people (v. 20)? What kind of men was Moses to select as judges of the people (v. 21)? What was Moses' response to the wise counsel he received (vv. 24-25)?

- 1 Samuel 23:2—What did David do before going to battle against the Philistines (cf. Ps. 16:7)?

- 1 Kings 12:6-20—What wise counsel did King Rehoboam receive (v. 7)? What evil counsel did he heed (v. 13-14)? What was the result (v. 19)?

- Jeremiah 32:19—What kind of counsel does the Lord give? How is that possible?

- Psalm 19:7-11; 119:130—What provides trustworthy counsel?

2. Through the well-meaning words of Peter, Satan was craftily setting a baited trap. The Lord's swift and strong response to Satan and Peter is an example to heed. Puritan Thomas Brooks offered this scriptural advice in his *Precious Remedies Against Satan's Devices*: "Keep at the greatest distance from sin, and from playing with the golden bait that Satan holds forth to catch you. . . . It is our wisest and our safest course to stand at the farthest distance from sin; not to go near the house of the harlot, but to fly from all appearance of evil. . . . Joseph keeps at a distance from sin, and from playing with Satan's golden baits, and strands. David draws near, and plays with the bait, and falls" ([Edinburgh: The Banner of Truth Trust, 1987], pp. 30-31). Having learned about Satan's crafty schemes, Peter wrote, "Be sober, be vigilant, because your adversary, the devil, like a roaring lion walketh about, seeking whom he may devour" (1 Pet. 5:8). Be on the watch for Satan's baited traps!

3. Through suffering God refines us. Look up the following verses and write down the principles they teach about affliction.

    • Psalm 119:67; 2 Corinthians 4:17:

    • 2 Corinthians 4:1, 16; Revelation 2:3:

    • Job 23:10; Isaiah 48:10; 1 Peter 1:7:

    • Deuteronomy 8:5; John 15:2:

Scripture Index

Topical Index

MacArthur, John
  his airplane conversation
      with a drinker, 23-25
  his not wanting to build
      the church, 20
Maurois, André, relativism
      of, 30
Messiah, the. *See* Jesus Christ,
      messiahship of
Monod, Jacques, relativism
      of, 30

Passover, the, 14-15
Peter
  confession of, 7-18, 33-34
  presumption of, 48-53
  as a rock, 32-35

Relativism, 30
Resurrection
  Christ's, 47
  promise of, 35
Ryle, J. C., on Christ's build
      ing the church, 27-28

Sabbaths, understanding the
      various, 14-16, 18

"Safe in the Arms of Jesus."
      See Crosby, Fanny
Salvation, rest of. *See* Sabbaths
Sartre, Jean-Paul, relativism
      of, 30
Satan, deceitfulness of, 53
Scripture, authority of, 36-37,
      39
Sin, deceitfulness of, 53
Son of God. *See* Jesus Christ,
      sonship of
Stone, Samuel J., his hymn
      "The Church's One
      Foundation," 38-39
Suffering
  resisting, 48, 51
  responding to, 48, 51

Trials. *See* Suffering
Tabernacles, Feast of, 15
Trumpets, Feast of, 15

Unleavened Bread, Feast of,
      14-15

Watson, Thomas, on the
      Word's authority, 39